THE COLLECTOR'S WORLD OF M&M's

AN UNAUTHORIZED HANDBOOK AND PRICE GUIDE

Patsy Clevenger

4880 Lower Valley Road, Atglen, PA 19310 USA

DEDICATION

I would like to dedicate this book to the M&M's Company for their great candies and their wonderful M&M's characters.

ACKNOWLEDGMENTS

I would like to thank all my friends and family for their help. A special thank you to: Millie Dowell, Edna Hilley, Karen Gifford, Lizabeth Rutan Rumenapp, Heinz W. Rumenapp, Sue Crane, and everyone at the M&M Mars.

Copyright © 1998 by Patsy Clevenger
Library of Congress Catalog Card Number:
  97-80155

Book Design by: Laurie A. Smucker

ISBN: 0-7643-0406-2
Printed in China
1 2 3 4

Published by Schiffer Publishing Ltd.
4880 Lower Valley Road
Atglen, Pa 19310
Phone: (610) 593-1777
Fax: (610) 593-2002
E-mail: schifferbk@aol.com
Please contact us for a free catalog.
This book may be purchased from the publisher.
Please include $3.95 for shipping.
Try your book store First.

We are interested in hearing from authors with book ideas on related subjects

Contents

PREFACE

M&M's Chocolate Candies continue to be one of the most popular candies. Naturally, collecting memorabilia of the sweet soon followed. All it takes is one M&M character to get you started—their smiles are absolutely infectious.

In 1993, I entered a little shop containing collectibles and spotted a 1992 brown peanut Easter M&M topper. Its smile just reached out and grabbed me, so I grabbed it. Two weeks later, at a garage sale, I found two more in a "free" box. Undecided what to do with them, I placed them on my dresser. The next morning when I woke up and looked at the toppers, they made me smile. Their smiles are contagious. I decided a smile was a great way to start the day so the toppers stayed and the search for more started. It is not unusual for me to travel a hundred miles for a new find with another smiling face to add to my collection.

In February of 1996, when the *FX Collectors* show from New York was filming in Longview, Washington, my friend, June Trusty, called them to suggest they feature my M&M's collection on their show. About two weeks later the show was broadcast nationwide from the parlor of my home.

I thought that I was the only M&M's collector out there, but after the broadcast I received letters and phone calls from New York, New Jersey, Florida, Nevada, Oregon, and Washington. M&M's collectibles have extended my world and my friends to different parts of the United States. With each new find we call each other with excitement. If it's an older, hard-to-find item, photos are taken and mailed out. I am always amazed at each new item that is found.

Blow-up advertisement item, 31 inches, 1995. $15.

M&M's History

True Colors

M&M's got their start with two men—Forrest Mars and a man named Murray—in 1940. At some point Murray sold out, thus giving us Mars, Incorporated.

During World War II, servicemen found M&M's in their ration pack. Women at the USO also passed them out to the servicemen.

M&M's first came out as a brown chocolate candy coated peanut. In 1950 they started printing a black "M" on the candy. In 1954, they changed to the white "M" because it stood out more.

M&M Characters were first used in television commercials in the early 1960s, with pipe cleaner arms and legs, with their face behind the "M." They have changed over the years.

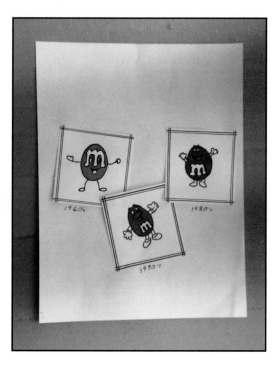

In response to a nationwide scare over red dye in 1976, all red M&M's were removed from the market, even though the dye was tested and FDA approved. In 1984, red M&M's once again appeared in the packages.

In 1984, green M&M's were the rage with teenagers when a rumor spread that they were aphrodisiacs.

In 1988, the M&M company introduced almond candy for the holidays. Mint M&M's came out the following year for Christmas.

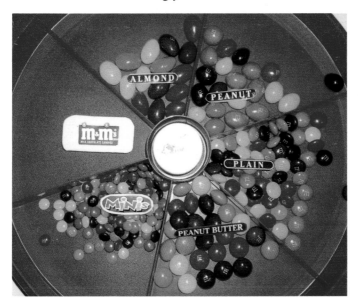

There are now a variety of M&M candies. My favorites include almond, peanut, plain, peanut butter, and minis, including children's minis, semi sweet bits, and milk chocolate bits.

Some of the M&M non-food items on the market were not authorized by Mars, Inc. even though these products are marked Mars, Inc.

M&M's Timeline

1940—Brown chocolate covered peanuts; M&M's introduced in the original colors: red, green, brown, orange, and yellow soon after.

1985—Red and green colors for Christmas.

1986—First pastel colors.

1990—Harvest colors.

1990—Pastel mints introduced for Easter, carried until 1993.

1991—New Valentine M&M's in red and white; 1992 in pink and white; 1993 in red, white, and pink.

1992—M&M's come out as brightly colored baking bits.

1992—Red, white, and blue candies released for the Fourth of July. Due to lack of interest in these colors, Mars only made them for three years.

1995—The new blue color is in the news after a contest in which it beat out pink and purple.

1995—First Halloween colors, brown and orange.

1996—In October, M&M Mars announces the arrival of the new twenty-four color pack.

Dispensers

These brightly colored M&M's dispensers are made of hard plastic and have a cheerful smile. They are M&M Mars approved. Red peanut, 1992; yellow European, 1992, and green pocket peanut, 1991.

Peanut 3.75-inch-tall pocket dispensers. On back is a twist plate to fill with candy, 1991. $4-5 each.

In January 1997, Burger King came out with M&M's pocket dispensers in their Kids Club Meals. Also included was a Fun Size bag of plain M&M's. Here is Burger King's plain red M&M's in an inner tube. To fill, put candy in the back of head. Candy comes out the back of the inner tube. $4.

Burger King's peanut blue M&M playing saxophone. There is a hole in the back of head to fill. Tip forward, candies come out the end of the saxophone. $4.

Plain 3-inch-tall pocket dispensers also have a twist plate for filling them with candy, 1991. $4-5 each.

Burger King's yellow peanut M&M holds a lunch box. There is a hole in the back of the head to fill. Candy falls out of the lunch pail when rolled across the table. $4.

Burger King's plain green M&M in a purple car. There is a hole in the back of head to fill. Candies come out the back of the car. $4.

Burger King's orange peanut M&M in dump truck. The candy goes in the bed of the truck. The bed tips to dump candy out. $4.

Red and yellow plain pocket dispensers (came with a four-inch plastic floral bowl marked "FTD"), 3 inches, 1992. $5-6 each.

M&M's gumball dispenser, 9 inch, 1992. $7-10.

These dispensers fasten to your belt; push a button on the back of the dispenser and candy is automatically dispensed, 1996. $5 each.

Large green, plain dispenser, 8.5-inches tall. This color is difficult to find, 1992. $18-20.

Large yellow dispenser, 10 inches, 1991. $15-18.

Large red, plain dispenser, 8.5 inches, 1991 or 1992. $15-18.

Large red peanut dispenser 10 inches, 1992. $15-18.

Large red peanut football player dispenser, 9inches, 1995. $15-18.

Large blue peanut basketball player dispenser, 13 inches. Not dated, but came out in 1997. $15-18.

Large orange plain baseball player dispenser, 10inches. Not dated, but came out in 1996. $15-18.

Red skier and yellow skier are both European peanut dispensers. 6.5" tall. 1991. $30 each.

European red, plain soccer player dispenser, 6.5-inches tall, 1991. $30.

European yellow peanut weight lifter dispenser, 6.5-inches tall, 1991. $30.

European plain yellow Easter dispenser. 6.5-inches tall, 1992. $30.

European plain green Easter dispenser, 6.5-inches tall, 1992. $30.

TINS

M&M Mars has come out with bright and cheerful tins. They make a nice collection.

This 1986 M&M's tin came in plain and peanut. The small banner under the first M on the lid indicates whether it is plain or peanut. Also, the inside circle is yellow for peanut, brown is plain. This tin closely resembles the 1988 peanut tin. The lid is the easiest way to tell the difference. The tall tin from 1986 measures 6 inches, the short one 2.5 inches. $4. each.

The banners on the lids indicate the year and plain or peanut.

In 1988 and 1989, the M&M's tins were purple with M&M's in the sky in place of stars. The silhouette varies a little. The tall one is 6 inches, the short one 2.5 inches. $4. each.

Peanut on left, plain on right. They also came in 2.5-inch size. $4 each.

This lid helps to distinguish it from the 1986 issue.

This 1988 tin is not dated. It was sealed in plastic with a sticker that indicated the date.

This July 4th tin is very patriotic with it's colorful design. The tins are 6 inches tall, 1988. $4 each.

M&M Mars came out with a 50th birthday tin. This tin is peanut and has three individual pictures on it, 6.8 inches, 1990. $4.

M&M's peanut holiday tin, 1991. The lid and bottom have a
paper cover. Contained only green and red candies. $7.

Both sides of the 1991 Christmas tin. Plain or peanut was indicated on the lid, 6.5 inches.
$4. each.

This shows another side of the 1990 50th birthday tin, showing the first M&M's characters, $4; and Christmas tin with children dreaming of M&M's, 5 by 7 inches, 1991, $8.

M&M's tin with winter scene on back side: plain, 1991, and one peanut, 1992; both 6.5-inches tall. $4.

Plain Christmas tin, 1993, 6.5 inches. $4.

1993 Christmas tin with Santa cooking 6.75 inches; 1994 Christmas tin with Santa and the M&M's characters in his workshop, 6.5 inches. $4 each.

Peanut Christmas tin, 1993, shows the playful M&M's characters, 6.5-inches tall. $4.

Post office, 1995, plain, 6 inches. $4.

1995 bed and breakfast, peanut, 6.5 inches. $4.

Toy shop, 1996, plain, 6 inches. $4.

Diner cafe, 1996, peanut, 4.75 inches. $4.

TOPPERS

These cute little guys are the lids for cardboard tubes that held M&M's candy.

Toppers came in both plain and peanut. They are wearing Santa hats and came in red, green, orange, and yellow. 1988. 2.25"-2.5". $3 each.

Toppers came in both plain and peanut. They wear Santa hats and ice skates. They came in red, green, orange, and yellow, 1989, 2.25- 2.5 inches. $3 each.

Toppers came in both plain and peanut. They are wearing Santa hats. They have a snowball in each hand and a pile of snowballs on the base. These toppers came in red, green, orange, and yellow in 1990. 2.25- 2.5 inches. $3 each.

These plain and peanut toppers wear Santa hats and are on skis. They came in red, green, orange, yellow, and brown, 1991. $3 each.

M&M's came out with two red peanut toppers in 1991. The only difference is the bottom part of the ski pole, which was either red or black.

The Olympic toppers came out in 1991 and 1992. Each event represented came in plain and peanut. There was only one color for each of the seven different events. The torch bearer was red; the hurdler and hockey player green; the weight lifter and ice skater orange; and the soccer player and skier were yellow. All have a square base. $5 each.

Valentine toppers came out in both plain and peanut. They have wings and carry a bow and arrow. They came in red, green, orange, yellow, brown, and pink, 1992-95. 2.25-2.5 inches. $4 each.

Easter toppers came out in both plain and peanut. They stand on a green base with a basket of eggs on the base and an egg in their left hand. They came in red, green, orange, yellow, and brown, 1992. $4 each.

These two are European toppers. Both are dated 1992 and both have a square base. $7.

Toppers came in both plain and peanut. They wear a Santa hat and hold a candy cane; red, green, orange, yellow, and brown, 1992. $3 each.

Plain 1993 and 1994 toppers wear a Santa hat and come out of the chimney, red and green only. The peanut toppers wear a Santa hat and sit on a sled, red and green only. $3 each

These 1994 Easter toppers came in plain only. The M&M's are in an eggshell on a green base. They came in pastel shades of pink, green, lavender, and blue; 2.25 inches. $3 each.

1994 and 1995 Easter toppers came in peanut only. They stand on a green base, holding a paint brush and a chick. These came in pastel colors of pink, green, lavender, and blue; 2.5 inches. $3 each.

42

M&M plain with train on the base, red and green, 1995, 2.25-inches tall. $3 each. M&M peanut with song book in hand, red and green, 1995, 2.5-inches tall. $3 each.

Valentine toppers came only in plain. They are mailmen who hold letters in their left hands and a heart-shaped candy box in their right hand. They came only in red or pink, 1996, 2.25 inches. $3 each.

1996 Easter toppers came only in plain. They stand on a green base with a watering can in their left hand and a flower in the right hand. They came in pastel colors of pink, green, lavender, and blue, 2.25 inches. $3 each.

1996 peanut toppers came in green, holding a snowball and wearing a stocking cap. Also, plain toppers were red, on a snowboard wearing a stocking cap, 2.5 inches. $3 each.

TUBES

Valentine topper and cardboard tube. Tubes change, just as the toppers change, for each season, 1996. Topper, $3; tube, $2.

Tube and topper, 1992. Tube, $5; Topper, $3.

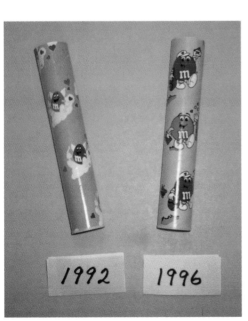

Valentine tubes, approximately 9 inches. Left, 1992, $5; right, 1996, $2.

The Olympic tubes were square, 1992. Topper, $5; tube, $5.

Easter tubes. Left, 1995, peanut; middle, 1995, plain; right, 1996, plain or peanut. $2 each.

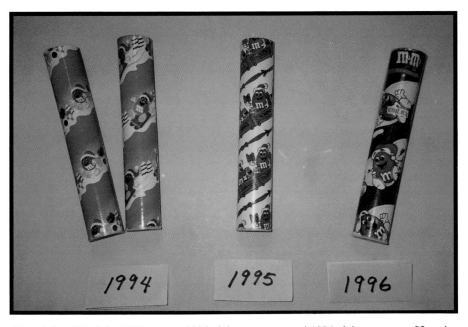

From left: 1994 plain, 1994 peanut, 1995 plain or peanut, and 1996 plain or peanut. $2 each.

TOYS

Assorted M&M's stuffed toys.

Pogs. These were in between the M&M's
cardboard fire truck bed and the boxes of
minis, 1995, 50 cents each.

Pogs, 1995. 50 cents each.

This fun cutout was on the back of the box
that the Fun Machine, or gumball dispenser, came in.

Assortment of stuffed M&M's characters. They range in size from 3 to 23 inches across and come in assorted colors.

Two, three-inch M&M's plush toy Fun Friends, 1994, Plain on left, peanut on right. Available in red, green, orange, and yellow. $3 each.

Three-inch Fun Plush M&M's toys in purple, pink, and blue, dated 1994. They were part of a Mail-in offer in 1995 during a contest to choose a new color for the candy. Blue was the winner. $3 each.

Four-inch, red stuffed Fun Friend "M" by Fun Stuffed, 1987. $3. Also, 4-inch yellow stuffed "M"s were made by Ace. $2.

This 3-inch, lavender M&M's rabbit with a basket of eggs was given to participants in the 1996 Picture Perfect Photo Contest. The winner received a family reunion for twenty people in Walt Disney World. $5.

This 7-inch, plain character was made by ACE Novelty Co. $2.

Seven-inch red and blue character with plastic eyes. The little red character is three inches, dated 1994. All three were M&M Mars approved. Large, $12; small, $3.

Three-inch Santa Claus M&M's stuffed toy came in red or green, 1994. $6 each.

The 8-inch green character on the left has plastic eyes and is an M&M's Fun Plush toy. The 6-inch green character on the right is by ACE. Left, $12; right, $2.

These 2.5-inch, hard plastic bears have a fuzzy fur covering. They are classified as Merry Miniatures made by Heartline. $10 each.

Matchbox came out with this Super Rig. The detachable trailer is yellow and has two M&M's characters sliding down a stream of chocolate. Yellow truck, 1983, and trailer, 1991. $5 for both.

Tennis ball with plain red character playing tennis. $4.

"All the World Loves M&M's" stickers, 1986. $1 each.

Circus stickers made by Ambassador, four
sheets to a package, 1986. $2 a sheet.

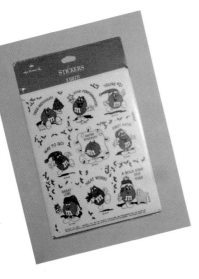

Christmas stickers by Hallmark, 1994. $1
per sheet.

Stickers, 1995. $1 per sheet.

Cardboard fire truck, 1995. $4.

Christmas stickers that were found in the
1996 M&M's Minis cardboard Santa Sled
with Mini boxes, 1996. 50 cents.

Individual mini boxes from the fire truck.

1993 Book, *The Missing Christmas Present,* came in a package with a small, 1.5-inch plain red M&M character and a small package of M&M's. On the back of the package is a game board. The book is 6.5 inches tall. $3 book, $4 character.

Cardboard bunny truck, loaded with ten mini boxes, 1997. $4.

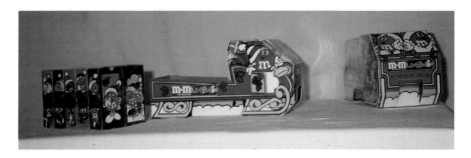

Cardboard Santa sled and ten individual mini boxes, 1996. $4.

Both of these books are dated 1994. However, the top book has a blue M&M in the word "Counting," so we know that it came out in 1996 or later. $7 each.

The first pages in counting books are different. The top photo is of the book with the blue M&M.

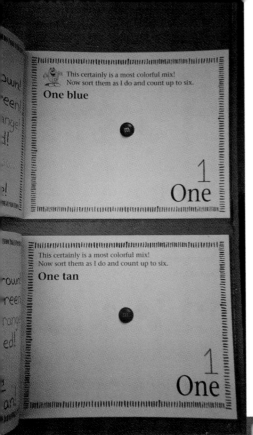

Page 6 of counting book provides another example of differences between the two books. The newer book has added M&M's characters to it.

Game board. This is the cardboard backing to the book, *The Missing Christmas Present*, 1993.

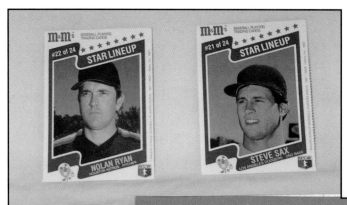

Two baseball cards, front and back, from 24-card set, 1987. $2 per card.

Game page from February 1996 *Nickelodeon* magazine.

KITCHEN

These cute little 2.75- and 3-inch refrigerator magnets were sold as a fund-raiser project in 1996. $7 for three-piece set.

Bear refrigerator magnets wearing M&M's shirts, 1984, from Mars, 2.5-inches tall. $4 each.

Red plain M&M's cookie cutter, 3-inches tall. Not dated. $5.

Assorted kitchen items.

Recipe cards, 3 x 5, purchased from a fundraiser. Each card features an M&M's character, 1996.

Half of a dishtowel, made into a hand towel, from 1996 fund-raiser. $7.

"Bake with the Best" pot holder from Mars, Inc., 1986. $8.

Cookbook, 5.25 by 8.25 inches, November 19, 1996. $4.

Festive Favorites recipe folder features colorful edibles for the holidays, 3.5 by 8.5 inches, Mars, Inc., 1986. $1.

Label from a canister, 1996.

In 1995, some magazines carried manufacturer's coupons with an attached recipe.

Bake'n Make cookbook features M&M's cookies. A tear-out insert, 5.5 by 9.25 inches, no date. $2.

Brighter Baking cookbook, dated 1994, 5.5 by 8.5 inches, 16 pages. $2.

Mars came out with a Holiday Wreath recipe in 1996. $1.

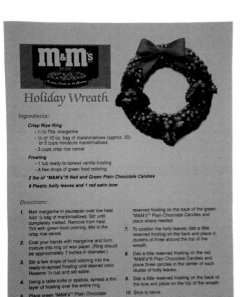

"Fun & Easy" recipe sheet, undated. $1.

This Pyrex football bowl is 5.75 inches across. It has the M&M's logo plus red, green, and orange players, all peanut characters, undated. $8.

This 4.75-inch bowl by Diamant has decal with white lettering "M&M's Peanut Butter Chocolate Candies." $5.

Front and back of the 1980s Olympic jar. Front has two M&M's characters holding a United States flag. Below that it reads, "Mars, Inc. 1983." On back it says "1980 L.A. Olympic Committee, Games of the XXIIIrd Olympiad, Los Angeles 1984," 8 inches tall. $3 with no stickers on lid or bottom.

This picture shows the plain and peanut M&M's labels on the lids of the 1980s Olympic jar. $5.

SCHIFFER PUBLISHING LTD
4880 LOWER VALLEY ROAD
ATGLEN, PA 19310-9717

WE HOPE THAT YOU ENJOY THIS BOOK AND ... ... your library. We would like to keep you informed about other publications from Schiffer Publishing Ltd.

TITLE OF BOOK: _____

☐ hardcover
☐ paperback

☐ Bought at: _____
☐ Received as gift

COMMENTS or ideas for books you would like us to publish. _____

_____

Name (please print clearly) _____

Address _____

City _____ State _____ Zip _____

☐ Please send me a free Schiffer Arts, Antiques & Collectibles catalog.
☐ Please send me a free Schiffer Woodcarving, Woodworking & Crafts catalog
☐ Please send me a free Schiffer Military/Aviation History catalog
☐ Please send me a free Whitford Press Mind, Body & Spirit and Donning Pictorials & Cook books catalog.

Telephone: (610)-593-1777   Fax: (610)-593-2002   E-mail: Schifferbk@aol.com

SCHIFFER BOOKS ARE CURRENTLY AVAILABLE FROM YOUR BOOKSELLER

Jimmy Dean came out with a snack pack
that contained Pizza, Cheetos, and plain
M&M's in 1997.

Godfather's Pizza came out with an 8.5-
inch M&M's dessert pizza in 1997.

Pillsbury M&M's cookie dough, 1996.

The 1996 Kudos bars had M&M's mini candies in them.

1996 Kudos' wrappers. The top one was early 1996. At the end of that year, an M&M's character was added to the wrapper.

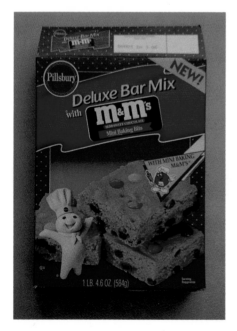

In 1996, Pillsbury introduces Deluxe Bar Mix with M&M's semi-sweet chocolate mini baking bits.

Oscar Mayer came out with a Lunchable
Fun Pack that included a small, Fun Size
bag of M&M's in 1996.

This Santa's Candy House Kit box shows the cute little M&M's characters building the
house. The box is 14 by 18.5 inches with a white plastic carrying handle, 1996.

Doug Clevenger assembles the M&M's house.

M&M's Candy Holiday House is a cardboard structure, covered with icing, and decorated with candies. It requires five pounds of M&M's, Skittles, Milky Ways, and Snickers. Everything needed came in the house package, 1996.

Party Favors

Mars, Inc. authorized the production of party supplies and seasonal items through the Hallmark Company to mark M&M's Mars fiftieth anniversary in 1990.

M&M's party hat with Mars, Inc., from Hallmark, 1993, by Party Express. $3.

M&M's cup and party invitation, Mars, Inc., from Hallmark, 1993, made by Party Express. $3 each.

M&M's 6.5-inch napkin, $2 each; and 7- by 6-inch treat sack, $4 each. Both are marked Mars, Inc., from Hallmark, 1993, and made by Party Express. Five-inch napkins also available in same design, $2 each.

M&M's 9- and 7-inch paper plates marked Mars, Inc., from Hallmark, 1993, made by Party Express. $3 each.

M&M's paper tablecloth marked Mars, Inc., from Hallmark, 1988, 54 by 102 inches; by Ambassador. $18-20.

M&M's paper tablecloth marked Mars, Inc., from Hallmark, 1993, 54 by 89.25 inches, by Party Express. $8-10.

JEWELRY

Set of six Olympic pins. All plain characters: Green speed skating, red free-style skating, orange ice hockey, brown gymnastics, yellow soccer, and red track and field. On back of each pin is "Mars, Inc. 1981. 36 USC 380 official Mark, Canadian Olympic Association." $15 for set.

Close up of Olympic Speed Skating pin, 1981. $2.

Small M&M's brand chocolate candies' hat pin.

Little yellow plain M&M pin with red Santa cap. $4.

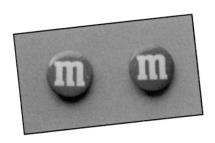

Pin backs in pink or purple, 1 inch. $2.

Watch with a red M&M character on a skate board. 1995. $15.

50th Anniversary watch with red plain character wearing a party hat. 1990. $15.

Watch with brown background with colorful M&M's on bottom half. 1987. $15.

Watch has a blue
character playing a
saxophone. 1996. $15.

1996 M&M's Fun Watch offer.

Front and back of T-shirt, no date. $12.

Cara Buswell, 15, in her M&M's Halloween costume, made from Simplicity pattern #9895 by her mother, Renee Buswell, in 1996.

M&M's sunglasses and case. Glasses have a yellow M&M character sticker on them and M&M's safety shoestrings. The case looks like a bag of peanut M&M's on one side and plain M&M's on the other side, Mars, Inc., 1988. $12.

Red and black baseball cap with mini M&M character, 1997. $6.

White painter's cap with red striping, 1988. $3.

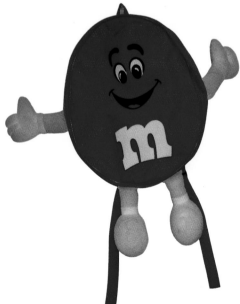

M&M's backpack, red with white "M." $20.

Red cooler bag with large white "M," 8 inches across, 1996. $5.

White shirt with red stripes. Left sleeve reads "Grab on to that M&M's feeling," right sleeve has a colorful stream of plain M&M's, 1988. $15.

White M&M's T-shirt. On the front is, "All the world loves M&M's," with assorted characters playing basketball, and on the back is, "The milk chocolate melts in your mouth—not in your hand." $15.

Posters

M&M's 9- by18-inch poster, undated. $4.

Burger King poster made of plastic showing M&M's dispensers, 1997.

Poster showing Burger King's M&M's dispensers, 19.5 by 19.5 inches, 1997.

"Melts in Your Mouth" poster, 17 by 22 inches, 1994. $5.

Poster reprint of a 1942 advertisement, 27 by 12 inches, 1987. $12.

Poster made from a 1995 wrap-around, 25 by 30 inches. $15.

Poster made from a 1994 wrap-around, 25 by 30 inches. (Wrap-arounds are plastic sheets about 20 feet long made to go around a cardboard box display). $15 for each.

Cardboard Count Dracula, 72.5 by 43.5 inches, dated 1995, from Universal Studios Monsters. $40.

Yellow cardboard peanut M&M with Christmas packages, wearing Santa hat, 22.5 by 19 inches, 1993. $5.

Red cardboard plain M&M with Christmas packages, wearing Santa hat, 18.5 by 18 inches, 1993. $5.

CHRISTMAS LIGHTS

Strings of M&M's Christmas lights and replacement bulbs.

These Christmas lights included a 6-ounce bag of M&M's peanuts, 1993. $9.

Christmas lights in original M&M's colors; red, green, yellow, and orange, 1994. $9.

Replacement reflectors and bulbs, 1996. $2.

Holiday Christmas lights in red and green, 1996. $9.

Christmas lights include the "New Blue" character, 1996. $9.

Miscellaneous

M&M's key chains made of PVC, 2.75-inches tall, circa 1980s, unauthorized. I only know of plain characters in red, green, orange, and yellow. $8-10 each.

Hallmark offered this 2-inch, plastic Christmas tree ornament in 1988. Date and Mars, Inc. on back. Available in green, red, and orange. $8 each.

M&M's red plastic clock, battery operated, 16 by 9 inches. The bottom of the clock face has "Mars, Inc. 1979." This clock is missing its M&M's pendulum, $25; in mint condition, $50.

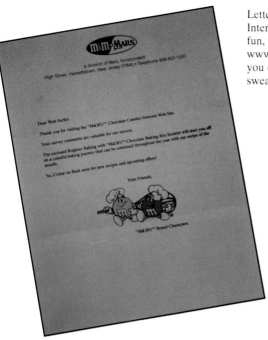

Letter from M&M's Chocolate Candies Internet Web Site. For information or just fun, visit their web site at www.http://www.m-ms.com. The site has a store where you can order items such as hats, sweatshirts, T-shirts, and more.

Mars came out with "Basket Treats" for Easter in February 1997. The basket treats are a hollow milk chocolate treat with M&M's plain candies inside; 3-inches tall. Could be bought individually or in a box of three.

Hollow chocolate eggs with Fun Size bags of plain M&M's inside. The Canadian version of the chocolate egg was inside a gold plastic shell and the box has French writing on it, 1996. Box and shell, $7.

M&M's plastic red heart music box. The pink M&M Valentine character on top is hinged. When lifted to stand, it plays *Let Me Call You Sweetheart*. 5.6-ounce bag of plain M&M's inside. Only color known available, "Mars, Inc. 1991" on bottom, 7 by 6 inches. $10-16.

Plastic Mickey Mouse Head candy box, 7 inches from ear to nose, 1989. $12.

What is it? This 1940s piece made of wool is 4 by 6.5 feet. It was bought in the Portland, Oregon area. The seller claimed that it was an M&M's candy banner for conventions. There is some doubt.

Korea's candy-coated, chocolate-covered peanuts, 1996.

These two characters are pillows. They are made from nylon material and are 12-inch circles. $12 each.

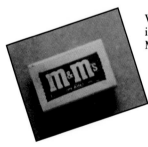

Wooden rubber ink stamp. If you use brown ink, it looks just like a mini bag of plain M&M's. $6.

This book cover shows the cute M&M's Minis at play, 14.5 by 22.25 inches, 1996. $2.

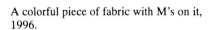

A colorful piece of fabric with M's on it, 1996.

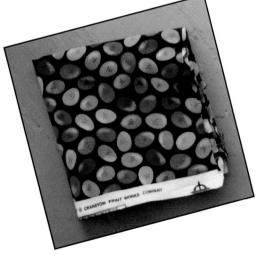

Two 4-inch FTD plastic flower bowls and dispensers. The company delivered a bouquet and, suspended from wire hangers, a bag of plain M&M's, the dispenser, and an FTD card with M&M's characters on it. Red and yellow only, 1992. Bowl $4, Dispenser $4-6.

Simplicity's pattern #9895 is found in the costume section of pattern books.

In 1995, Cannon came out with these colorful M&M's bedding items. Sheets $20-40, Comforters $40-50, Shams $20, and Curtains $30.

Rabbit plant sticks, unauthorized. $1 each.

Plastic case has a .999 fine silver coin in it. It has the M&M character in birthday hat, blowing a horn. This was made in celebration of Mars, Inc. 50th anniversary, 1990.

Car sun shield, 20.5 by 42 inches, dated 1988. $12.

110 Keystone Camera with carrying bag, one side of carrying case resembles bag of plain M&M's, other side peanut M&M's. $25.

M&M's EVERYWHERE

Tag from M&M's Character Fun Friends, 2.25 by 2.25 inches.

Business in Centralia, Washington. Building has 7-foot high M&M's characters painted on windows, 1997.

A 3-foot high M&M character painted on the side of a house in Centralia, Washington, 1997.

Display in Centralia Antique Square, Centralia, Washington, February 1997.

Located in a store, red plain and blue peanut. Both stand about 43-inches tall. Red is dated 1994, blue 1996. $10 each.

These two cute M&M's characters were found on a truck dashboard, 1997.

McGill and Lincoln in a pose for the "Picture Perfect Basket" M&M Mars photo contest 1996. *Photo by Greg Anderson.*

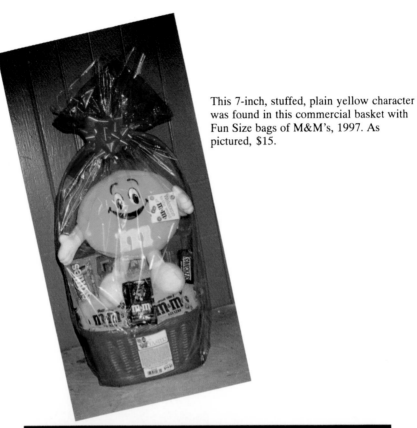

This 7-inch, stuffed, plain yellow character was found in this commercial basket with Fun Size bags of M&M's, 1997. As pictured, $15.

Two more commercial baskets with stuffed M&M's characters. The red one is peanut and the green is plain, 1997. As pictured, $15 each.

M&M's in an Easter basket (or bucket) sold in stores, 1997.

ADVERTISEMENT ITEMS

Plastic advertisement piece hangs from the display rack and bounces, 7.5 by 11 inches, 1997. $3.

"New Blue" plastic advertisement piece hangs from the display rack and bounces, 6 by 8 inches, 1996. $3.

Advertisement balloon, 17.5 inches, dated 1993. $4.

Advertisement balloon, 17.5 inches across, dated 1993. $4.

Advertisement balloon, 17.5 inches, dated 1995. $4.

Cardboard advertisement for Dairy Queen, 5 by 5 inches, 1996. $2.

In 1995, Mars., Inc. held a contest to introduce a new color to their candies. The choices were purple, pink, blue, or no change. At the same time, you could mail for a free 3-inch, mini plush character. With each order you had to enclose the color you wanted, proof of purchase, and $1 for postage.

This is the back of a consumer coupon. It shows Mars varieties available, 1995.

Advertisement for school bus, 1995.

Burger King advertisement folder with a game board inside, 1997. $1 each.

PACKAGING

Colorful 1996 Valentine packages held Fun Size packs with "To:" and "From:" on the back.

Christmas mint package, 1995.

Christmas packages: Top plain, bottom, peanut, 1995.

Cardboard Valentine heart with plain candies, 6-inches tall, 1995.

Box of 6 individual gift boxes for Valentines Day, 1995.

M&M's package introduces the "New Blue" color, 1995.

Small M&M's peanut candy box, 3-inches tall, 5.75-inches long, 3.5-inches wide, 1990. $6.

A rare old box which the M&M's archives can't date. No price available. *Courtesy of Kay Hurd. Seattle, Washington.*

Large plain M&M's box with red character on one side, lime-green character on the other side, no date.

Large peanut M&M's box with orange character on one side, green on the other, no date.

DISPLAYS

This flat box has holes in it to stand tubes for easy display, 1996.

Music box display, held eight music boxes. On top in front is a white "Press Here" sticker. When pressed it plays *Let Me Call You Sweetheart*, 1997.

Fund-raiser variety box with plastic carrying handle, 1996.

Cardboard display for the toy shop in 1996 Christmas Village. Flat, 2-inch tall box.

Colorful, wedge-shape box held pink cardboard hearts, 1995.

Each mini candy box becomes a dispenser. With the shoot open, tubes roll out freely, 1997, box is 4.5 by 10 inches.

The 1997 Basket Treats box for single characters.

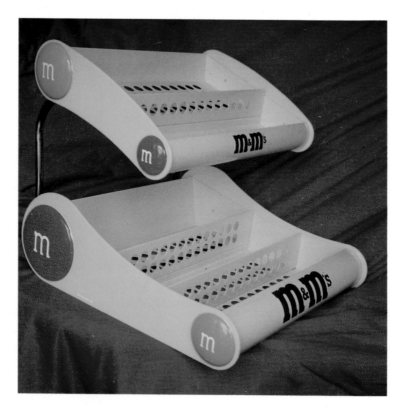

Table top display rack. Rack is metal with a colorful plastic M&M's on each end, 15-inches tall, 18-inches long, 18-inches wide, 1997. $35.

This cute poster is on the top of metal rack approximately 6 by 4 feet. $45.

Five-shelf, metal display rack with red plain character and green peanut character, approximately 42-inches tall. $35.

Cardboard floor display unit for "New Minis." Each unit held eight boxes; the four boxes on the top could be opened at same time, approximately 4-feet tall, 1997.

Most Wanted display is cardboard and held
boxes of M&M's candy, 1996.

Cardboard barrel display, six sided. Filled
from top with individual bags, 1997.

116

Older metal floor rack with wheels for easy moving. Has five removable or adjustable shelves. Side advertisement piece is pressed wood.

Cardboard floor display for the M&M's school bus. Two boxes fit into the display, twenty-four buses to each box. Each box has eyelet holes to mount on the wall if desired, 1996.

LIZ'S COLLECTION

The following photos are from the collection of Lizabeth Rutan Rumenapp. The photographs are by Heinz W. Rumenapp of Oneonta, New York.

M&M's fund-raiser hats, 1988. $5 each.

Minis Christmas sleigh with display box, 1996.

School bus box. Top two rolls are fire truck trucks. Two middle rolls, school buses; bottom rolls, Easter trucks.

Side view of bus, sleigh, rabbit, and fire truck.

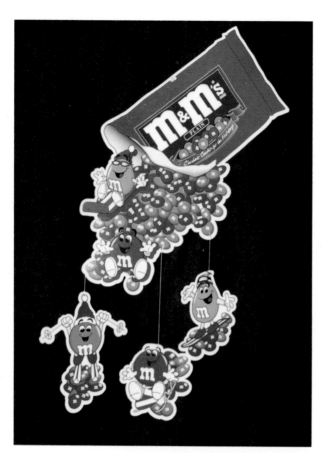

Christmas display mobile, 1996. $5.

Green Santa M&M's character floor display, 41 by 49 inches, 1996. $10.

Red cardboard floor display, 42.5 by 34 inches. $10.

Blue cardboard floor display, 41 by 34 inches, 1996. $10.

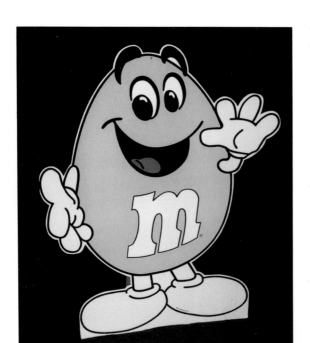

Yellow cardboard floor display, 49 by 42 inches. $10.

Cardboard display, 17 by 13 inches, 1995. $5.

122

These items were purchased through a fund-raiser, December 1996. Memo board 9.75 by 11 inches, $9. Grocery pad, $7.

Fund-raiser items, 1996. From left: utensil holder, 5-inches tall, $13; coffee cup, $15; recipe box and cookie cutter, $14, and other side of utensil holder.

Save the Children fund-raiser tin and 13-inch stuffed character, from the 1996 *Bloomingdale Winter Catalog*. $49.

M&M's Levi jacket with character on back.

Magnets, purchased from fund-raiser, 1996. $7. per set.

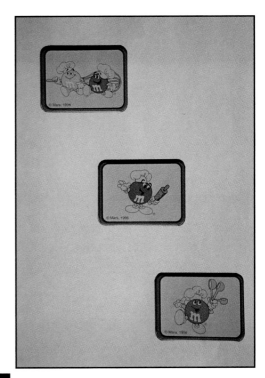

M&M's costume with 3-inch stuffed characters attached. Stuffed toys $3 each, costume $15.

Sheet of wrap-around for the 1996 campaign "Fun in the Sun," with matching umbrella.

"Fun in the Sun" T-shirt, 1996. $12.

White T-shirt with yellow and red characters. $12.

Christmas ornaments made from Polystone, from fund-raiser, 2-inches high, 1996. $7 each.

Plastic picture frame with M&M's around the outside, 1996. $5.

To introduce the new cooking candies, this
tin came with semi-sweet candy for baking,
a cookie cutter, and cookbook. Set $9.

Ballpoint pen, Salesman's sample. $5.

Bear paper clip, 3-inches tall. $3.

Plastic travel glass, 8.25-inches tall, 1996. $6.